Loved from Eternity

Loved from Eternity

D. E. YOUNG
Foreword by Stephen Jennings

RESOURCE *Publications* • Eugene, Oregon

LOVED FROM ETERNITY

Copyright © 2017 D. E. Young. All rights reserved. Except for brief quotations in critical publications or reviews, no part of this book may be reproduced in any manner without prior written permission from the publisher. Write: Permissions, Wipf and Stock Publishers, 199 W. 8th Ave., Suite 3, Eugene, OR 97401.

Resource Publications
An Imprint of Wipf and Stock Publishers
199 W. 8th Ave., Suite 3
Eugene, OR 97401

www.wipfandstock.com

PAPERBACK ISBN: 978-1-5326-0595-6
HARDCOVER ISBN: 978-1-5326-0597-0
EBOOK ISBN: 978-1-5326-0596-3

Manufactured in the U.S.A.   JANUARY 31, 2017

Contents

Foreword by Stephen Jennings | ix

On Romans 9:3 | 1
On the Burial of Jesus Christ | 1
Vanity | 2
But the Greatest of These is Love | 3
On the Marriage of a Friend | 3
Canticles 8:6, 7 | 4
For the Rev. Dr. Henry
   Krabbendam | 4
The Unintended Blessing of
   Balaam | 5
Naaman's Maid | 6
On Folks Joining the Church | 7
Hosea | 8
On Alexander Pope's Essay on
   Man | 9
For Mrs. David Smith, on Her
   Death at 92 Years of Age | 9
On the Curse: Thorns and
   Thistles | 9
Intercession | 10
A Secret Athlete | 10
Hebrews 2:16 | 11
The Thorn in the Flesh | 12
On the Death of D.B. | 12
My Legacy | 13
Spiritual Insomnia | 13
Unsinkable | 14
Liar | 14
Imagine This | 14
Bear Ye One Another's Burdens | 15
Inverse | 15
On the Cancer of a Friend | 15
The Perfect Church | 16
On the Attire of the High
   Priest | 16
Thy Will be Done | 17
For Buttons, a Dachshund | 17
II Corinthians 5:21 | 18
Dawn | 18
On An Expected Cancer
   Diagnosis | 19
To Our Lord Jesus Christ | 19
Heidelberg Catechism Lord's Day
   19 | 20
Dawn (II) | 21
For Elizabeth Joy, Not Yet Born | 22
Grace (III) | 22
My Treasure, to L.M. | 23
He Shall Sit With Me Upon My
   Throne | 24
A New Name | 24
I Corinthians 15:49 | 25
For Bear and Autumn, on Their
   Deaths a Few Days Apart | 25

Contents

After Autumn | 26
For Elizabeth Joy, Not Yet Born (II) | 27
From II Corinthians 3–5 | 28
Recompense (II) | 30
Intercession (II) | 30
Perspective (III) | 31
On The Rare Jewel of Christian Contentment | 31
On The Widow's Mite (II) | 32
For Elizabeth Joy, Not Yet Born (III) | 33
On the Genetics of the People of God | 33
On Standing Before Christ | 34
On a Friend Moving Away | 34
Lot's Choice | 35
Isaiah 50:6 | 36
A Secret Soldier | 36
Pressure | 37
Chastisement (IV) | 37
Genesis 15:1 | 38
From Psalm 37:13 | 38
Father, Forgive Them | 39
On Philippians 1:29 | 40
Transformation | 40
From Psalm 27 | 40
Poem, Written on the Road | 42
Isaac | 42
Isaiah 63:9, 16 | 43
I Peter 2:18–25 | 43
Before the Throne | 44
Looking Heavenward | 45
Abraham, Isaac, and Jacob | 46
Moses | 46
For Elizabeth Joy, Not Doing Well | 47
A Secret Justice | 47
Monday Morning, Returning to Work | 48
Prayer | 48
On The Burial of Abraham | 49
The Lion of the Tribe of Judah | 50
Jacob Have I Loved, But Esau Have I Hated | 50
Because He Loved Her | 51
Earth Day 2014 | 51
For Elizabeth Joy, Gone to Heaven | 52
For Meriam Ibrahim Ibshag, Sentenced to Death for Christianity | 52
Boolean Logic 101 | 53
"When I am Weak, Then am I Strong. . . ." | 54
Job 6:12 | 54
Help | 54
Lesson from Laban and Jacob | 55
On Yearning for the Celestial City | 55
Prayer | 56
From Psalm 22 | 56
From I Peter 4 | 58
The Mercy Seat | 58
At the Table (III) | 59
Salt of the Earth | 59
For a Certain Deacon | 59
For a Certain Deacon (II) | 60
For MB | 60
My Treasure (II) | 60
Facing Death | 61
Security | 61
Covenant | 61
Psalm 147:11 | 62
Isaiah 37:35 | 62
Poem for Bear, Hunting Mooses in his Dreams | 62
The Key of David | 63
On Psalm 37 | 63
On Matthew 7:21–23 | 64
My Father, My King | 64
A Secret Boxer | 65
From Psalm 144 | 66
On Getting Old | 66
Submission (II) | 67
On Matthew 5:43–48 | 67
On Fallen Humanity and Plastic Plants | 68
On Leviticus 10 and I Corinthians 11 | 68

Contents

Affliction (V) | 68
Joseph | 69
Outcry | 69
Justice | 69
I John 3:18 | 70
II Corinthians 8:9 | 70
Colossians 3:2-4 | 71
The Good Samaritan | 71
From Hebrews 12 | 72
Into Your Hands | 72
Most Gladly Therefore Will I Glory in my Infirmity | 73
Grace is a Diamond | 73
Psalm 70 | 74
I Corinthians 13:4 a | 74
They Hated Me Without a Cause | 75
Secret Soldiers: Hymn Version | 75
II Kings 9:26 | 76
II Kings 6:16 | 76
On Being in the Fiery Furnace Again | 77
Hebrews 5:8 | 77
I Kings 22:34 | 77
Job (IV) | 78
II Kings 19:14 | 78
From Psalm 25 | 78
Exodus | 79
Psalm 28 | 79
Grace (IV) | 80
Meekness and its Reward | 80
His Yoke is Easy | 81
A Lesson From Bandit | 81
I Must Have It | 82
Behold, He Prays | 83
Luke 18:1 | 83
Battle Cry | 84
I Samuel 21:1 | 84
The Last Day | 85
Built Upon the Cornerstone | 87
Romans 7:24-26 | 87
Acrostic Poem | 88
Christ, the King of His People | 89
And the Books Were Opened | 89
Psalm 69 | 89
Luke 7:36-45 | 92
Psalm 70 | 93
Perseverance (II) | 93
Fear Not | 94
Coram Deo | 95
A Bruised Reed Will He not Break | 96
On Seeing Birds Fly | 96
Menorah | 96
The Comforter | 97
Samson | 98
How Long? | 98
Hear my Cry | 99
From John 15 | 100
From Psalm 56:8 | 100
From Deuteronomy 8:2-4 | 100
From Hebrews 11:32-38 | 101
From Revelation 6:15-17 | 102
From Genesis 4:10,11 | 102
From James 5:10, 11 | 103
For the Rev. Dr. Robert Paul Martin | 104
On the Pharisee and the Publican | 105
The Last Day (II) | 105
Beside a Death Bed | 106
So Teach Us to Number Our Days | 106
Small | 106
For the Rev. Dr. Robert Paul Martin (II) | 107
Trust (II) | 107
For C.P. | 109
Hope (II) | 109
Genesis 18:25c | 110
Psalm 119:50 | 111
Pilgrim Starts Out | 112
The Last Enemy | 112
I Samuel 3:18 | 113
Genesis 15:1 | 113
Death Knocks | 113
Psalm 119:117 | 114
East | 114
Noah | 115
Regarding J.I. | 116

Contents

Pitch | 116
Contrast | 117
From Luke 16 | 117
Smokerise | 118
Advocate | 119
Asa | 119
Sapphira | 119
The Last Day (III) | 120
The Birth of Joy | 121
Consider the Lilies | 121
Grace | 122
Behold the Lamb | 122
From Exodus 1 | 123
O Ye of Little Faith | 124
On Seeing a Father Comfort a Crying Child | 124
What Love is This? | 125
The Real Superhero | 125
How Long? | 126
Veil | 126
Orlando | 127
Isaiah 40:30–31 | 127
Light of Glory | 127
Shake Well | 129
Hebrews 5:8 | 129
Crossing the Red Sea | 130
Luke 18:1–8 | 130
Compassion | 131
Canticles 6:3 | 133
Intercession (II) | 133
Egyptian Gold | 134
Love | 135
Wilt Thou Go With This Man? | 135
Show me Your Glory | 136
For Robert Samuel Dyer | 136
Fruit | 137
Adoption | 137
From Psalm 46 | 138
Greater Love | 138
The Tenth Commandment | 139
Proverbs 30:8–9 | 139
Peace, Be Still | 139
Timekeeping | 140
Quietness | 141
For Robert Samuel Dyer (II) | 141
Provision | 141
Unbelief Trampled | 142
Subdued | 142
On Christian Education | 143
Looking Upwards | 143

Foreword

Recently in the worship of God and with His people gathered on the Lord's Day, we prayed in song these words, so beautifully expressing the Gospel, fittingly communicating back to the Savior His own teaching that "Blessed are the poor in spirit, for theirs is the Kingdom of heaven; blessed are those who mourn, for they shall be comforted, blessed are the meek, for they shall inherit the earth, blessed are those who hunger and thirst for righteousness, for they shall be satisfied." (Matthew 5:3–6)

> Not worthy, Lord! to gather up the crumbs
> With trembling hand that from thy table fall,
> A weary, heavy-laden sinner comes
> To plead thy promise and obey thy call.
>
> I am not worthy to be thought thy child,
> Nor sit the last and lowest at thy board;
> Too long a wand'rer and too oft beguiled,
> I only ask one reconciling word.
>
> One word from thee, my Lord, one smile, one look,
> And I could face the cold, rough world again;
> And with that treasure in my heart could brook
> The wrath of devils and the scorn of men.

Foreword

> I hear thy voice; thou bidd'st me come and rest;
> I come, I kneel, I clasp thy pierced feet;
> Thou bidd'st me take my place, a welcome guest
> Among thy saints, and of thy banquet eat.
>
> My praise can only breathe itself in prayer,
> My prayer can only lose itself in thee;
> Dwell thou for ever in my breast, and there,
> Lord, let me sup with thee; sup thou with me.
>
> (Edward H. Bickersteth, 1872; The Trinity Hymnal, #428)

And I was reminded of Dorothy.

It is the philosopher, who from his place in academia, prescribes the big, but complicated ideas, that would rule in the minds of men. But it is through the artists-the screen writers, the music lyricists, the authors and poets, that those ideas reach the masses of common society. That is why Dorothy's gifts with words are so necessary for our souls. She is not composing for herself; she writes for all of us—"weary, heavily laden sinners who would plead His promises and obey His call."

I thank the Savior for Dorothy. She sat in our congregation as one who hungers and thirsts for righteousness, who gratefully ate at the King's table, and departed satisfied. (Shall I also recall that she was one who on Wednesday evenings at our home generously brought the food that refreshed our physical appetites?) No stranger to "the wrath of devils and the scorn of men," she knew that she has a "place," and is "a welcome guest among God's saints and of His banquet may eat."

Having come to Jesus, like the Syro-Phoenician woman with exemplary faith (Matthew 15:21–28), she shares with us her travails of soul and the "rest" that comes to those who have "taken His yoke and learned from the One who Himself is meek and lowly of heart" (Matthew 11:28–30). I urge you to listen for His voice speaking in these faith-offerings composed for the sake of His bride, the church. May you know that He fills those who have been emptied.

Rev. Dr. Stephen Jennings

On Romans 9:3

What Moses could not suffer,
what Paul could wish, not do,
for this, my soul, bless Jesus
Who was cut off for you.

A sinner cannot answer
for any other man,
but He Who bore our sorrows,
He has, He will, He can.

January 2012

On the Burial of Jesus Christ

You suffered Him to die,
Your own beloved Son.
You gave Him up for us,
for every chosen one.
You did not let Him see
corruption or decay.
You made His suff'rings end
upon that awful day.

He was not cast aside
as if He had no worth.
He had a burial
within the kindly earth
which He Himself had made
and set upon its way,
in honor laid to rest
upon that awful day.

So will You end for those
whom You forever love
their shame and their disgrace
when they meet You above.
We will not suffer on
In agony alway.
But little time until
that glad, eternal Day.

For You will raise us up
in image like to Him.
And we shall see our God
apart from shadows dim,
forever like to Him
Whom we alone adore
To be with Trinity
forever, ever more.

January 2012

Vanity

(Ecclesiastes, Matthew 5:4)

Beneath the sun there is no hope,
no glory, no reward,
but higher up is life and peace
in heaven with our Lord.
A few short days of sorrow more,
a few more tears and sighs,
and we shall be with Him above
enjoying Heaven's Prize.

Eternal rest and peace and joy,
eternal blessedness,
for those who in their pain below
their Savior did confess
and to the end did persevere
in mockery of pain.
In self-abasement, these the Sad
received eternal gain.

January 2012

But the Greatest of These is Love

How strong is Faith and stalwart!
How vast is Hope and free!
But Love is still the greatest
of these, the greatest three.

January 2012

On the Marriage of a Friend

I did not think I'd live to see
this day become reality.
So hard this world, so sad and ill—
who would have guessed that grace would fill
the deepest, saddest voids that ache
with peace that love and kindness make.

October 29, 2011

Canticles 8:6, 7

How strong is Death, the murderer,
that sweeps all men away,
but just as strong is gentle Love
that can its force allay.

No flood can drown sweet Charity,
nor waters wash away,
nor can a man obtain her
or for her favor pay.

Beyond all price, enduring still,
the greatest of the three,
first Faith, then Hope, then Charity,
that shall forever be.

February 14, 2012

For the Rev. Dr. Henry Krabbendam

(From Psalm 92:14)

Now you are old, but glory shines
brighter and brighter on your way,
the evidence of Love Divine
which shall shine to the perfect day.

Mercy that's come to age, and faith,
peace, love, and virtue, hotly tried,
hope that's more near fulfillment now
than when your soul was justified.

About to feast on Heaven's joy
more than your little taste below,
still full of sap and very green
that shall eternal Glory know.

So shall the cold, refreshing chill
of Grace from Heaven streaming down,
quench the hot, fiendish fires of Hell
with Mercy flowing all around.

February 2012

The Unintended Blessing of Balaam

How can I curse when God has blessed
His very own, though vile and weak
In their own selves, yet strong in Him
The mighty, holy, and the meek.

I see him from the highest rocks,
God's Israel dwelling safe below,
A sprawling city, tent on tent,
That shall eternal Glory know.

Who can the dust of Jacob count,
A quarter of their army see?
O let me die like one of them,
A righteous end give Thou to me!

This people all shall dwell alone,
No other folks shall venture nigh.
No unclean soul may enter in
Unto the holy city high.

For God has sworn to bless His own
Who will not change His holy will,
Who cannot lie like sons of men,
But will His purposes fulfill.

In Israel He sees no sin,
No wickedness and evil will.
Shouts of the King are in his camp,
And God will bless his dwelling still.

How fair thy dwelling, my belov'd!
How good thy tents all spread abroad!
No longer bound in slavery
But dwelling ever with thy God.

March 2012

Naaman's Maid

(II Kings 5ff)

I would I were like Naaman's maid,
The little captive unafraid
Who would her captor's blessing see
More than her own sweet liberty.

No faith the king had like the child,
In Providence she rested mild,
Content to serve, a captured slave,
And longed the mighty man to save.

Her faith a fearsome valor knew,
And so the weak, the poor, the few
Can topple battlements so high
When stronger folk dare not draw nigh.

This little maid, so poor and mean,
Beheld the warrior made clean.
Her faith a blessing was to those
Whom in eternity God chose.

If Providence should seem to frown
Let me embrace the thorny crown
And know that He works all things well
Who has redeemed my soul from Hell.

March 2012

On Folks Joining the Church

Come ye sheep and come ye lambs
Out the darksome night and cold
To the Gentle Shepherd's arms,
To the safety of the fold.

Strong the wolf's ferocity
And the lion's threatening roar,
You beside your mighty King
Shall be safe forevermore.

Fed and sheltered, safe and warm,
Free and freer yet to be,
Nestling in the refuge sure,
You shall Christ's protection see.

April 2012

Hosea

(From Hosea and Romans 9–11)

He loved her, and He married her,
Though she would faithless prove to be.
He took her for His own again
In matchless grace and mercy free.

Those that rebelled were not His own,
No mercy could for them be found,
But He redeemed them for Himself
And made them stand on holy ground.

Not only Jews, but others too,
A wild olive's fruitless tree,
Engrafted into covenant
That unto Him their fruit should be.

And God shall plant her in her place
Where she shall grow forever more.
What love is this bestowed upon
The weak and wicked, vile and poor?

Blest be the faithful God of Grace,
Beyond imagination kind,
Who paid Himself the awful price
That He His wand'ring ones might find.

April 2012

On Alexander Pope's Essay on Man

Look not alone on earth's bare fruitless span,
Nor fail the Holy Word in faith to scan,
Nor unto wretched humanism nod,
The proper study of mankind is God.

May 2012

For Mrs. David Smith, on Her Death at 92 Years of Age

She honor graciously retains,
The tribute that to her pertains,
Of mercy lover, and of truth:
'Tis well your given name is Ruth.

May 2012

On the Curse: Thorns and Thistles

The Scripture says work is accursed.
I think there's something to it.
If bother is the thing you want,
Most likely, thistle do it.

July 2012

Intercession

As Abraham before besought for Lot Your grace,
As Moses intervened before Your blessed face,
As Amos pled for Jacob, because he was so small,
The images of Jesus, Who pleaded for us all,
So we in measure tiny when for the lost we pray
Thus image our Redeemer Who by Himself would pay
The price of our redemption, to make us sinners good:
Our privilege and honor, if in the gap we stood.

August 2012

A Secret Athlete

(Honoring Eric Liddell, who would not run on the Lord's Day
for love of his King, against the wishes of his king.)

I am a secret athlete
Though no one else might know.
I have a race to finish,
Must win, not place or show.

But unlike other athletes
I am not strong at all.
Debilitating weakness
Is mine since Adam's fall.

Though newly recreated
By Spirit all Divine,
Yet sin around besets me
Although new life is mine.

What hope have I of glory,
Before His face to stand?
Just that my mighty Savior
Upholds me with His hand.

So though the flesh may bother
And frailty cling to me,
I shall arrive in Heaven
For Jesus strengthens me.

Eternal weight of glory
Exceeds Olympic gold,
And that shall be my story
When my last day is told.

August 2012

Hebrews 2:16

He does not help the angels
By strengthening their hands
As they fly at His bidding
Or follow His commands.
He gives help to His people,
Descendants of His friend,
The children born of promise,
To us He help will send.

August 2012

The Thorn in the Flesh

It sticks! It pokes! It bothers me,
Reminder of the Fall.
God sent it through Hell's agency
To keep my puffing small.

If I felt not my weakness
Nor heard my thoughts so snide
I might think I were better
Than those I walk beside.

I want my sin to wither
And die upon the vine,
But not till Heav'n's glory
Will perfect peace be mine.

And yet in this my weakness
I shall great power know
For He that sent Affliction
Shall also Mercy show.

August 2012

On the Death of D.B.

I know you heard the Gospel,
From my own lips you heard.
At least upon your outer ear
Did sound the faithful Word.
I wish I had some reason
To think you found your way
Unto the only Savior.
It would have made this day

On which you met your Maker
More easy for your friend.
But God knows what He's doing,
And all things have an end.
I hope we meet in glory,
Both snatched from out the flame.
I hope you found your comfort
In Jesus' holy name.
But God knows He's doing.
To Him I bow the knee.
I hope you found the Mercy
Alone which comforts me.

August 2012

My Legacy

Let me so live that when I die
All men may know the reason why
My God I treasured most of all,
For Mercy saved me from my Fall.

August 2012

Spiritual Insomnia

Why do You send me agony?
How is my suff'ring gain?
It's easier to stay awake
When one feels bitter pain.

August 2012

Unsinkable

O ye of little faith!
Why do ye doubt and fear?
Storms cannot sink the ship
When Christ the Lord is near.

August 2012

Liar

Between God and the Devil
Who told the truth, who lied?
"You shall be as the Highest"?
Or else "he died, he died"?

August 2012

Imagine This

If you would stretch your vision
Imagine if you can
The glory of our Savior,
The only Righteous Man,
Forsaken of His Father
For wretches such as I,
Denied, condemned, and dying
Beneath a darkened sky
My guilt and sorrow bearing,
The theanthropic man,
That I might be forgiven:
Imagine if you can.

September 2012

Bear Ye One Another's Burdens

If it weighs upon you, brother,
It shall weigh upon me too.
If my Lord has borne my burden,
Then I must bear yours with you.

September 2012

Inverse

(From Romans 14)

If you think love is lawless,
What are you dreaming of?
To love is to fulfill the law,
To keep the law, to love.

September 2012

On the Cancer of a Friend

How awful and tragic is cancer!
I hope against cancer we win,
But more than a world without cancer,
I long for a world without sin.

September 2012

The Perfect Church

If you the perfect church should find
Keep this one thought before your mind:
If joining it you should think fit,
That deed would surely ruin it.

September 2012

On the Attire of the High Priest

Engrave me on the onyx stones
That shall upon Thy shoulders be.
Engrave me on the precious gems
That on Thy heart the world shall see.

For Thou didst bear my name on High
Before the Judge and Majesty
When Thou didst offer up Thyself,
A Ransom and a Remedy.

Who am I, Lord, that Thou should'st love
The weak and wretched, vile and poor,
That Thou should'st give Thyself for me
That Thou my ruin might restore?

Blest be the Father's mighty Love,
Blest be the Savior's Mercy free,
Blest be the Spirit, earnest given
That I Thy blessed Face shall see.

October 2012

Thy Will be Done

(I Samuel 3:18)

Lord, let Thy will be done
Whate'er Thou dost ordain,
In peace and happiness and joy,
In sorrow and in pain.

O glorify Thy name
E'en when we know not how.
Submissively before Thy throne
Thy chosen people bow.

The priest of old discerned
'Twas not Thy will to save,
But when Thy glory did depart
He lay down in his grave.

Before the awful tree
Did agonize Thy Son,
But still submissively He prayed,
"Thy will, not Mine, be done."

October 2012

For Buttons, a Dachshund

Sleep, little friend, from care set free.
Know you were precious unto me.

No pain or sorrow more to know,
Where grief and anguish cannot go.

If God on sparrows spends His care,
In His safekeeping you must share.

Know you were loved entirely.
Sleep, little friend, from care set free.

November 2012

II Corinthians 5:21

Blest be my Jesus, made for me
My Sin that I might righteous be.
He bore my sin when Justice pressed,
Else were my sin Mount Never-Rest.

November 2012

Dawn

I was in prison lying,
A dark and bitter place,
Until there shone upon me
The brightness of Your Grace,
A lightning bolt of Mercy
Across my midnight sky,
A rising dawn of radiance,
That I might live thereby,
The Glory of my Jesus,
Your Mercy and Your Grace,
That I might live forever
To gaze upon Your Face.

November 2012

On An Expected Cancer Diagnosis

Now it shall not be long
Till I shall be with Thee.
Now it shall not be long
Until Thy face I see.

A little more to strive,
A day to persevere,
Till I be free from sin
And see Thee in the clear.

Welcome, Death's bitter wave,
For when it washes o'er
Safe shall I find myself
On Heaven's blessed shore.

November 2012

To Our Lord Jesus Christ

You Who did wear the thorns for me,
And You Whose side was pierced for me,
O make Your anguish for my guilt
The sure death of my sin to be.

If I behold Your mighty love,
Your mercy, rich, profound, and free,
Make Grace the Rock that breaks the heart
That from Your side would often flee.

Be unto me both Death and Life
That mortifies the sin in me
That I may see Your Blessed Face,
Forever pure, from sin set free.

February 2013

Heidelberg Catechism Lord's Day 19
Question 52: Answer

In my distress I lift mine eyes
Unto the heavens high
And wait for Him to come to judge
Who bore my agony,
Who stood for me before the throne
Of Righteous Majesty,
Condemned and sentenced for my sins
For which I ought to die.
And the whole curse has swallowed up;
Who will His foes destroy
And my foes too, though all His own
Shall reign with Him in joy,
Forever gazing on the Face
Of Grace beyond compare,
Forever prostrate at His feet
For Mercy rich and fair.

February 2013

Dawn (II)

Making Request for Unconverted Friends

O let the darkness flee!
Let firstborn light begin
To shine in these dark hearts!
Drive out the night of sin.

Let these the Glory see
In Jesus' Blessed Face:
The Glory of our God,
Your free and matchless Grace.

O You Who made the light
Your first command obey,
Let these before You live!
O give the light of day!

Have mercy on the lost!
O bring the strangers near!
O let the dead arise
When they the Gospel hear!

Stretch forth the Arm of Strength,
And make the kingdom grow,
That hopeless, helpless men
May Life eternal know.

February 2013

For Elizabeth Joy, Not Yet Born

Sweet babe, so tiny still
That may not live to see
The light of life on earth
Instead, Eternity.

God knows why He has made
Your frame so feebly small.
He formed you in the womb
To show His glory all.

Your parents bow the knee
To God's almighty will
For you to live or die
And wait upon Him still.

Let nature wail for you,
Small child. Let rain descend.
Let all things weep for you,
See what shall be your end.

Will God His mercy show
And grant you yet to live
Or take you to Himself
And greater mercy give?

February 2013

Grace (III)

I hated You, but You loved me
Almighty Sovereign Majesty,
And not content that I should die
You laid Your crown of Glory by,

A servant's humble form to wear,
Our human misery to share.
You bore such anguish and distress
The depths of which I cannot guess.
Your Father's outrage at my sin
You bore that You my soul might win.
Almighty Mercy, Boundless Grace,
That I might gaze upon Your Face!
I bless the Father, Spirit, Son,
My Priceless Treasure, Three in One.

April 2013

My Treasure, to L.M.

My Treasure sits upon
The universal throne,
And He takes for Himself
The ones He calls His own.

So take your place and pride,
Your ease and leisure too,
Your rank and fame and power
For I have more than you.

My God is my delight
And He deigns to love me
For reasons of His own.
Yours is the poverty.

April 2013

He Shall Sit With Me Upon My Throne
(Rev 3:21)

What is this You, my Lord, have said
That we shall sit upon Your Throne,
Where You in splendor and in grace
Rule o'er the world that is Your own?

For we are weak and vile and poor
And You are holy, Mighty Three.
And yet You call us to draw near,
To sit enthroned with Trinity.

To see Your face were grace enough,
Your throne alone with peace to see.
To sit with You upon Your throne
Is mercy in infinity.

April 2013

A New Name
(Rev 2:17)

The name my parents gave me
I bore so oft with shame
But when You come in glory,
You'll give me a new name.

It shall remain untarnished
As endless ages roll
For I shall then be perfect
In body, mind, and soul.

April 2013

I Corinthians 15:49

I look just like my father,
The first rebellious man,
But thanks to grace and mercy
According to His plan,
I shall be like my Savior,
His image bear at last,
When death has worked me over
And this sad world is past.

Or when He comes in glory
In twinkling of an eye,
Made like unto my Savior
No more to sin or die,
When Death is dead forever,
And there is no more grave.
Blest be the Second Adam
Who died my soul to save.

April 2013

For Bear and Autumn, on Their Deaths a Few Days Apart

Death is not part of life.
It was not "meant to be."
It is a thief crept in
To steal from you and me.

If we had not rebelled
In Adam long ago
We would not feel the pain
Of death or sorrow know.

But there is One Who bore
Our death and agony,
Who conquered Death Himself
And bore our misery.

He shall rebuild this world,
All things shall make anew.
And maybe these we loved
Shall see the new world too.

With Noah in the ark,
And by the Red Sea way,
God rescued animals
Through types of Judgment Day.

Perhaps these that we loved
Shall live again at last.
When this sad world is done
And when the Fire is past.

What God will do with them
I cannot venture more.
He will do what is right,
Of that we can be sure.

May 2013

After Autumn

(Genesis 9)

After Autumn comes the Winter
Deadly dark and cold.
After Winter comes the Spring when
Leaf and flow'r unfold.

After Springtime comes the Summer's
Scorching, blasting heat,
After Summer, gentle Autumn:
Cycle is complete.

So the Seasons circle onward
To the world's last day
Sent by common Grace and Cov'nant
His will to obey

That the Kingdom may grow upward
From the Gospel seed,
That the wretched may find refuge
In their time of need.

May 2013

For Elizabeth Joy, Not Yet Born (II)

You're a dancer, you're a fighter,
Yet to see a single day.

You are chosen, you are precious,
You are loved in every way

By your father, by your mother,
By your Savior most of all.

Precious baby, gift of heaven,
For your sake on God we call.

We shall storm the gates of heaven,
Beg that you may mercy see.

To the Father of all Mercies
By your life let Glory be.

May 2013

From II Corinthians 3–5

With open face beholding
The Glory of the Lord,
In Scripture's holy mirror
Where Gospel Truth is stored,
By that view ever changing
From what we used to be
To what through endless ages
Eternity shall see.

Though broken and discouraged
Yet fainting not at all,
Though dying while we're living,
Decaying through our fall,
Cast down, not to destruction,
Forsaken, not alone,
That life be manifested
When in the earth we're sown.

Our outward man may perish
And more and more decay
But still we press on upward
Upon the holy way.
Our transient affliction,
So heavy but so light,
Shall work eternal glory,
Not everlasting night.

We gaze upon the unseen:
Invisible, we see;
The things of sense and vision
Don't last eternally.
Our earthly tents still folding
Around us day by day,
And groaning for our future
We long to launch away.

To see His face in glory
Be done with death and sin;
Come, Death, and do your office
And let us enter in,
Or else if He come quickly
We shall be clothed upon:
Immortal then the mortal
In twinkling shall put on.

And we shall live forever
In permanent delight.
Though it may seem we stumble
We walk by faith not sight.
But if I had an option
I'd rather absent be
For then I'd be with Jesus
For all eternity.

June 2013

Recompense (II)

If for my pain, You give me, Lord,
The lives of these I love,
Instead of cursing You for grief
I'll praise my God above.

When rocks do fall on reprobates,
They curse You for their ill.
I will not curse: no, I will bless
And wait upon Your will.

If You should crush my feeble frame
With agony and woe
Still will I bow the knee to You
And meek to death will go.

Grant the intention of the heart
To You to bow the knee
Of fact a matter may be shown
And not a fantasy.

June 2013

Intercession (II)

If when Elijah prayed
The God of Heav'n gave ear,
What mercies shall be wrought
When He His Son shall hear?

If much when sinners pray,
How much when God the Son
For His bride makes request?
What wonders shall be done?

June 2013

Perspective (III)

Though I may think that I am poor
If I lack daily bread,
When You were here, You had no place
In which to lay Your head.

June 2013

On The Rare Jewel of Christian Contentment

Come, my soul, bow the knee
To Him Who reigns on high.
He has decreed your state
Himself to glorify.

Whether He little give
Or riches heaped above,
It is enough for you
That you enjoy His love.

If I have food to eat
And clothes that I may wear,
Let me contented be
With my God's tender care.

Riches are good and fine
Yet often to the soul
They stand to hinder it,
To bar it from its goal.

Let me seek Heaven first,
His face with joy to see,
If He will give Himself
I shall contented be.

July 2013

On The Widow's Mite (II)

He sat there and He watched her
Although she did not know.
He saw her give the last she had,
A selfless spirit show.

He saw she loved His Majesty,
His worship, house, and law.
It was not things He saw she loved
But Him, her Fear and Awe.

Who gave the greater gift, think you?
The rich who gave from ease
Or she who gave the last she had
Her mighty King to please?

Who got the greater blessing back?
Whose portion was not small,
From kind and mighty Providence
But hers who gave her all?

July 2013

For Elizabeth Joy, Not Yet Born (III)

Now comes the bitter hour,
Now comes the day
For you to come to birth
Or pass away.

God has been glorified:
Heaven and Hell
Have struggled in the womb,
And all is well.

If you should never see
Daylight at last
Still you shall glory know
When life is past.

Rest easy, little one,
Nor doubt nor fear.
God has His hand on you
And He is near.

July 2013

On the Genetics of the People of God

There is but one ethnicity
That shall behold His face:
It is the new humanity—
The family of Grace.

September 2013

On Standing Before Christ

I would fear to stand before Thee
Were it not that Thou hast died,
Bearing all my guilt and sorrow
In Thy hands and bleeding side.

For if Thou hast borne the burden
Which I could not lift or move
Wilt Thou not receive me gently
With the tokens of Thy love?

And though I am vile and needy,
Bad, perverse, benighted, poor,
Yet I look to Thee for mercy
And my soul needs nothing more.

I shall boldly come before Thee
On the dreadful Judgment Day:
By Thy living and Thy dying
Thou hast borne my guilt away.

For which bless I Thee, my Jesus,
And to Thee I bow the knee:
Blessed be Thy boundless mercy:
Bless'd be Holy Trinity.

September 2013

On a Friend Moving Away

Farewell, but not goodbye:
Be in God's tender care.
Be found in Christ at last
Though here you be or there.

Seek Him, the greatest good:
For Him all things forgo.
You must have Him at last
If you would glory know.

Feast on His mighty love:
Rest in His mercy free
For then you shall be safe,
For all eternity.

There's honey in the Rock:
The sweetness is profound.
Trust Jesus Christ alone.
In Him is refuge found.

September 2013

Lot's Choice

Lot chose him all the fertile plain,
A lovely piece of sod,
But Abram's prize was greater still
For his reward was God.

September 2013

Isaiah 50:6

"I gave My back to the smiters and My cheeks to them that plucked out
the hair. I hid not My face from shame and spitting...."

If You let hands that You had made
from Your cheeks pull the hair,
O give me grace the sins of these,
my foes and Yours, to bear.

September 2013

A Secret Soldier

I am a secret soldier,
a servant of the Cross,
ordained to pain and sorrow,
to agony and loss.

What cause have I to grumble
when You Who went before
deserving naught but blessing
instead my burden bore?

Shall flogging, mocking, spitting
deter me from the Way?
What hope had I of glory
had You turned back that day?

It is enough for servants
their Lord to imitate.
Give grace and strength and patience
upon my Lord to wait.

But Oh! The prospect precious
when conflicts all are o'er
to gaze upon the Victor
forever, ever more.

September 2103

Pressure

I am a pile of carbon
Beneath a mountain high.
I feel the weight upon me:
To pain I testify.

But what do weight and pressure
For carbon undertake?
From something poor and worthless
They will a diamond make.

September 2013

Chastisement (IV)

If You should smite me day by day
With mighty, chastening rod,
What does it say about my state
But I am loved by God?

September 2013

Genesis 15:1

If God should undertake
To shield my soul from harm
What foe can Him withstand?
Who has a stronger arm?

September 2013

From Psalm 37:13

"The Lord shall laugh at him...."

Laugh at my foes
who think they will
harm Your poor child,
destroy her still.

Or better yet,
in mercy great
rescue these folks
from their sad state.

Snatch from the fire,
who did me smite.
Grant them Your mercy
in Your might.

Let not the Foe
fulfill his will:
Save me and these,
I beg You still.

September 2013

Father, Forgive Them

"Forgive them, Father, they know not
the evil thing they do."
You spoke these words upon the cross
when they were killing You.
And Stephen begged for mercy too
for those that killed him all,
and in that mob there stood Your saint
at that time known as Saul

About to meet the risen Christ
Who did not like the way
His little ones were done to death
and intervened that day.
Upon the road where Saul breathed out
his rage and vile intent,
the risen Savior intervened
and saved him as he went.

So those that smite with evil will
perhaps may yet become
when You have risen in Your strength
those You will welcome home.
So give me gentleness and grace
to see beyond the wrong
and for their souls and Your great Grace
with all my heart to long.

September 2013

On Philippians 1:29

Of all the gifts that Mercy gives
For which we thanks should make,
The hardest to be grateful for
Is suff'ring for His sake.

Since He for us our sorrows bore,
Our burdens undertook
Then we beyond our little cares
To others' needs should look.

September 2013

Transformation

'Tis gazing at the Glory
That daily changes me
From what I was and what I am
To what I yet shall be.
Majestic, Sovereign Mercy
And Love beyond degree
Because of Grace Almighty
Are resurrecting me.

September 2013

From Psalm 27

My covenant God, He is my strength,
My life, my hiding place.
What shall I fear when God is near
And I behold His face?

What foe can rise and conquer me
If Sovereignty defend?
My foes that fain would eat me up
Shall meet instead their end.

I asked Him for just one great thing:
That on Him I may gaze
And see His beauty in His house
All of my earthly days.

He hides me in His secret place
Where war can't find or fear,
He sets me up upon a rock
And graciously draws near.

Therefore with joy I sing His praise
Among the gathered throng
Of saints all come to worship Him
In hearing, prayer, and song.

Hear, Lord, when I cry out to You,
Have mercy—O be near!
When You said to me "Seek Me"
My heart replied with fear.

O do not give what I deserve:
To never see Your face!
Do not in anger banish me
But save me in Your grace.

If Mother and if Father dear
Should cast my soul aside,
Yet You will hold me safely up
And will with me abide.

O give me not to them that hate,
Would see me in my grave.
I would have fainted had I not
Been sure that You would save.

So, my dear friends, wait for your God,
And on His grace depend.
For he that trusts in God alone
Shall have a joyful end.

November 2013

Poem, Written on the Road

If one should pray for gentleness
To grace and mercy show
I think that He Who reigns on high
Will likely not say, "No."

October 2013

Isaac

(Genesis 17ff)

Abram was old, Sarai was old.
What would their future be?
What would their aged arms embrace
But Laughter rich and free?
The Lord of Life Who laughs at death
And infertility,
The obstacles that no one else
Can overcome but He,

Since He has sworn the son should come
Though long their wait may be,
Life, grace, and mercy from His hand,
Yes, they shall surely see.

November 2013

Isaiah 63:9, 16

In my distress, You were distressed,
You shared my agony.
The only reason that I live
Is that You rescued me.

Though Abraham may know us not
Nor Israel us confess
Yet we are Yours, our Gracious God,
Our Father, do us bless!

December 2013

I Peter 2:18–25

He called us unto suff'ring
That we His steps should trace.
He called us to injustice
Before we see His face.
He called us to mistreatment,
To sorrow deep and grim,
That in our homeward journey
Our souls might follow Him

Who trusted God Almighty
To set all things to right,
To wait upon His rescue
All through the darksome night.

December 2013

Before the Throne

All shall be well with me,
Though weak and full of shame.
He reigns supreme on high
To magnify His name.

He reigns, and I shall live.
He reigns, what foe can smite?
He reigns in boundless grace
And in eternal might.

I stand before the Throne,
No higher seat can be.
What pow'r can overcome
The One Who shepherds me?

In Justice, Grace, and Power,
With Wisdom, Goodness, Love,
In Glory Infinite,
Our God Who reigns above.

January 2014

Looking Heavenward

O give me eyes to see
What I cannot behold,
The land of pure delight,
The citadel of gold.

My enemies are strong
They work their evil will,
They bask in luxury
And gnash upon me still.

How long must I go on
In deep distress and woe
Observing wicked men
In ease and comfort grow?

Lord, come and end this world,
This agony and pain.
Come bring Your kingdom in
Forever to remain.

Or take me there to You
Where I shall weep no more,
Give me instead of pain
Joy, peace, and comfort sure.

January 2014

Abraham, Isaac, and Jacob

God changed the name of Abram
To Abraham in peace,
And Jacob now is Israel,
But Laughter cannot cease.

February 2014

Moses

("For he endured as seeing Him Who is invisible. . . . ")

He saw Him Who's invisible,
Whom sinners cannot see.
It was that sight that held him up
In his adversity.

He chose reproaches, not the gold
Of the Egyptian store.
He chose to suffer with his Lord,
Esteeming suff'ring more.

So let me look beyond this world,
Intent on Glory gaze,
And let that sight make me endure
All of my pilgrim days.

February 2014

For Elizabeth Joy, Not Doing Well

So weary, little baby!
So hard your pilgrim way!
Rest on your Savior's bosom
Until the final Day!

Your short life brought Him glory,
Your hard road quickly past.
Rest now until the morning.
You shall I see at last.

February 2014

A Secret Justice

I am a secret justice
Though not a judge as yet,
Still waiting for the last Day
When earth its end has met.

I shall sit with my Savior
Upon His judgment throne:
I shall partake of judgment
Because I am His own.

In equity deciding
The fate of angels grim;
The wicked and the heathen
I shall condemn with Him.

My judgment shall be perfect:
I shall perfected be.
I shall decide with justice
For Justice I shall see.

No longer in the shadows
Or with beclouded eyes:
I shall be like my Savior.
I shall behold the Prize.

March 2014

Monday Morning, Returning to Work

Help, Lord, for I am weak:
I have no strength to stand.
I cannot bear abuse
From an unrighteous hand.

But You have borne contempt,
Brutality and scorn,
And that not for Yourself
But for Your saints that mourn.

Give, then, the Meek the land:
The Sad let gladness see:
O bring the kingdom in
That with You we may be.

March 2014

Prayer

Oh, do not give what I deserve,
That banished I should be.
Let me behold Your Glory, Lord,
Your mighty Majesty!

Your Grace profound and wondrous Love,
Your Goodness, Wisdom, Might!
Let me upon Your beauty gaze
Instead of endless night.

March 2014

On The Burial of Abraham

(Gen 25:1–18)

They laid him by his ancient bride,
She who so long he walked beside,
A symbol still of things to come
When all his sons are welcomed home,

A foretaste of the gath'ring sweet
When all God's sons before Him meet
With pain and sorrow fully past
To dwell in peace fore'er at last.

Machpelah's cave is not the end
For him who walked with God, his friend.
Death shall be swallowed up with life
For this great man and his dear wife.

April 2014

The Lion of the Tribe of Judah

(After Matthew Henry)

He Who for strength and might
Is called the Lion great
Has yet another name
That shows a different trait.

For mildness and calm,
For inoffensive mien,
This Lion is called Lamb
And that shall be His name.

Though mighty, bold, and strong
His people to defend,
It was as paschal Lamb
He met for us our end.

He judges, reigns, and rules
In mighty majesty,
But meekness is His crown
And shall forever be.

April 2014

Jacob Have I Loved, But Esau Have I Hated

The babies struggled in her womb,
Two sons, two nations, strong and great,
But Sovereignty chose one to life,
And left the other reprobate.

This choice of Sovereign Majesty
With myst'ry is indeed replete,
Not that He passed a sinner by
But that He loved the sneaking cheat.

April 2014

Because He Loved Her

As Jacob would for Rachel
Bear toil of seven years
So did our gracious Savior
For us bear pain and tears,
Tormented in His body
And in His soul distressed
That Justice might be sated
And that we might be blessed.
'T was all because He loved her
Would have her for His own—
And in the final glory,
His bride shall share His throne.

April 2014

Earth Day 2014

I love this place, sometimes at least,
To see the sun rise in the East,
The pleasant things that You have made,
The purple flow'r, the ev'ning shade,

But not from Earth Day is our bliss:
The Lord's Day bright was made for this:
Blest Sabbath Day, the best of seven:
Not made for earth but made for Heaven.

April 2014

For Elizabeth Joy, Gone to Heaven

You could not speak, and yet your sound
Has echoed all the earth around.
God has in you been glorified:
Now in His presence you abide.
Now comes the time, my little Joy,
For you your new voice to employ
To sing the praises of your Lord
By all the earth and heaven adored.
Rest, little friend, in His great love
For now you see Him up above.
And someday soon, we'll be with you
When all our pilgrim days are through.
To share His mighty love we thirst,
But you, our darling, got there first.

May 2014

For Meriam Ibrahim Ibshag, Sentenced to Death for Christianity

Be faithful unto death, my dear,
Not let your heart be sad or fear.
It may be He will rescue you
Or else give grace to bring you through

Your last great trial for His sake.
Beware that you do not forsake
For life the very Son of God.
'Twere better you should bear His rod
And stand before Him, sorrow past
Than gain the whole earth's treasure vast.
'Twere better you should face the flame
Than to blaspheme the Holy Name.

May 2014

Boolean Logic 101

If operands are joined by OR
And even one of them is true
This makes the statements wholly grand
For so the logic follows through.

But if by AND they should be joined
Then every one must truth be found
Or else the statement's wholly ruin'ed
For so the logic comes around.

You asked for logic. Here you are.
I'll bet that you are sorry now.
For logic's an exacting thing
And tells you what, not why or how.

But faith is supra-logical
That goes beyond the mind of man.
It grasps truths that cannot be seen,
That can't be measured in a can.

June 2014, at Pastor Jennings' instigation

"When I am Weak, Then am I Strong. . . ."

In my weakness I will boast:
In my pain and frailty,
For when I'm weak, I'm strong,
No foe can vanquish me
For the Might that keeps me safe
Is not mine but His alone.
His the Glory, His the praise:
Him my Rescuer I own.

June 2014

Job 6:12

What is my strength that I should wait?
Am I a rock or stone?
Lord, comfort me in my distress
And leave me not alone.

July 2014

Help

O give me grace that I may know
In wisdom what I ought to do
Lest left alone to my own mind
I do what will dishonor You.

July 2014

Lesson from Laban and Jacob

(From Genesis 31)

See what they do, my kindred foes
Who would their mother dispossess.
So hard their hearts and bitter souls
That still belief in Thee profess.

I pray Thee, Lord, in Providence
See what these people undertake,
And make the cattle, every one,
Bear spotted, speckled, and ringstraked.

July 2014

On Yearning for the Celestial City

When shall I be with Thee
And sorrow be no more?
When shall I cross the flood
Unto the peaceful shore?

When shall true friendship reign
And perfect equity?
When shall I Thee behold,
Forever bow the knee?

Fill Thou my soul with light.
I pray Thee let me see
As Moses saw of old
Thy matchless Majesty.

On Israel's praise enthroned,
In Holy Might and Power,
In Justice pure and high,
My God, my Strength and Tower.

July 2014

Prayer (II)

My Jesus, pray for me,
I beg You, intercede.
This trial is so hard:
Your grace and strength I need.

Guide my feet in the way,
Nor let me turn aside.
'Tis dark around me, Lord!
I pray You be my Guide.

August 2014

From Psalm 22

My God, why do You hide
Your blessed Face from me?
I cry by night, but You, my God
Are silent unto me.

I know that You are holy, Lord,
On Israel's praise enthroned.
Our fathers trusted in Your name,
And You their kinship owned.

I am a worm and not a man
Whom people do despise.
Reproached of men and laughed to scorn,
And worthless in their eyes.

They say You will deliver me
If in Your name I rest,
if truly You are pleased with me
and if perchance I'm blessed.

My God, I beg You, be not far
For there is none to save.
Strong bulls of Bashan circle me
And I draw near the grave.

My soul is poured out like a draught
My bones are out of place,
My heart is melted in my breast,
For I see not Your face.

For dogs have compassed me about,
The wicked all draw near,
They look and stare upon my soul
And mock me without fear.

My God, O do not stand afar.
I beg of You to hear,
O be my strength, come quickly, Lord,
And set me free from fear.

If You wilt save me then I shall
Your mercy freely tell,
The meek souls shall be satisfied
Whom You have saved from Hell.

I shall have a posterity
Though I alone may be:
And generations yet unborn
Shall know You rescued me.

August 2014

From I Peter 4

Because Your faithfulness
Is every morning new,
Because You're my Creator
That knows me through and through,
Because this pain is greater
Than I have felt before,
I pray You, gracious Savior,
To hear what I implore.
Give Grace and Strength and Courage
And Gentle Mercy Kind.
Enlighten me with Wisdom
And calm my troubled mind.

August 2014

The Mercy Seat

Disciples saw Your tomb
Where You had buried lain,
And on their solemn guard
The shining angels twain.

Why sat one at Your head,
The other at Your feet?
Because it was, in fact,
A very Mercy Seat.

August 2014

At the Table (III)

I pray You bid me take my seat
E'en at Your mighty board.
Though they are sweet, I've had enough
Of appetizers, Lord.

August 2014

Salt of the Earth

O make me in Your mighty Grace
Both sweet and salty be
That tasting me, my friends may taste
Of Your salinity.

August 2014

For a Certain Deacon

I can see Christ in you
In kindness and concerns
In fervor and in faith
And in a heart that burns

To know the God of Grace,
And Him to praise and love,
And you shall see His face
When we shall meet above.

August 2014

For a Certain Deacon (II)

You are blessed that you hunger
That you may more righteous be.
He who ever thirsts for goodness
Shall in fact that virtue see.

August 2014

For MB

Though you have taken what was mine,
With my goods you made free,
Yet still in fact you cannot steal
Inheritance from me.

August 2014

My Treasure (II)

If I should lose my earthly things
I will not shed a tear
For God is my inheritance.
My Treasure is not here.

August 2014

Facing Death

I come unto Your palace, Lord,
And Death stands guard before,
But every mighty fortress high
Has an imposing door.

August 2014

Security

Blest be my God Who keeps my soul
From injuries and harms.
Beneath my weak and fragile heart
Are everlasting arms.

August 2014

Covenant

(From Genesis 15)

I may have hope that I shall come
To Paradise at last
Because 'twas You between the parts
Of slaughtered creatures passed.

August 2014

Psalm 147:11

Come, be astounded, O my soul,
That such things can be true,
That Heaven's Mighty Monarch High
His pleasure takes in you.

August 2014

Isaiah 37:35

Come, Mighty Sovereign, us defend:
Protect the children of Your friend.
Rebuke the wicked that oppress:
And us with peace and mercy bless.

August 2014

Poem for Bear, Hunting Mooses in his Dreams

He'll be hunting lots of mooses when he comes;
He'll be hunting lots of mooses when he comes.
He'll be hunting lots of mooses
And be biting their cabooses,
He'll be hunting lots of mooses when he comes.

If he's hunting with Apaches when he comes,
If he's hunting with Apaches when he comes,
He'll be hunting lots of mooses
And be kissing the papooses,
He'll be hunting lots of mooses when he comes.

If he's living with the hermits when he comes,
If he's living with the hermits when he comes,
He'll be hunting lots of mooses
Though he's staying with recluses,
He'll be hunting lots of mooses when he comes.

He'll be catching lots of mooses when he comes;
He'll be catching lots of mooses when he comes.
He'll be catching lots of mooses
'Cause I don't accept excuses,
He'll be hunting lots of mooses when he comes.

March 2013

The Key of David

I may approach the Throne
And kneel to Majesty
For to the Throne Room high
My Jesus is the Key.

September 2014

On Psalm 37

Help, my God, deliver me
For I put my hope in Thee.
Save me from my foes unjust
For in Thee I put my trust.
Let not evil men prevail.
Let their ill intentions fail.

Break the bows with which they fight.
Save Thy servant in Thy might.

September 2014

On Matthew 7:21–23

O poor religious leaders
For some of you shall hear
Instead of welcome tidings
You may to Him draw near
Instead the sharp rejoinder,
Worst sentence that can be,
"Be gone, you wicked sinners.
I say depart from Me."

September 2014

My Father, My King

I praise You, mighty Maker,
To You my songs I bring,
My Sovereign and my Master,
My Father and my King.

September 2014

A Secret Boxer

I am a secret boxer,
A little punchy too.
It is myself that I must hit
Until my life is through.

Must bring me to subjection.
Must make myself obey
For to arrive in Heaven
There is no other way.

'Tis grace that drives me onward,
Against myself to strive.
'Tis grace for which I'm grateful
For grace keeps me alive.

Must pummel and must batter
Each sinful tendency.
Must put to death transgression
If I His face would see.

For I shall wear white garments
If I am black and blue
For only they who struggle
Are proven to be true.

October 2014

From Psalm 144

Blessed be the Lord my strength
Who teaches me to war and fight,
He is my goodness, my high tower
My shield, my trust, and my delight.

So what is man, Almighty King,
That you should knowledge take of him,
A puff of wind, a vanity,
Whose light grows ever dark and dim?

I pray You come from Heaven high,
To shoot Your arrows from above,
To put Your enemies to shame
Who vanity and falsehood love.

But I will sing unto my God
Who is my precious treasure store.
If God is mine, I have enough
And cannot ask for blessings more.

October 2014

On Getting Old

High or low, near or far,
Something hurts where'er you are.

October 2014

Submission (II)

My soul, commit your way
Into His mighty hands
Whom heaven and earth obey
And follow His commands.

He reigns inscrutable,
Nor can His ways be known
Except when He ordains
To show them to His own.

So pain and grief are yours?
Well, so are life and death.
Yes, all things are your own:
Joy follows your last breath.

November 2014

On Matthew 5:43–48

Because You love my soul
And gave Yourself for me
O grant me grace enough
To love my enemy.

November 2014

On Fallen Humanity and Plastic Plants

'Twixt plastic plants and living
One difference may be
That life has imperfection:
Life has deformity.

November 2014

On Leviticus 10 and I Corinthians 11

O grant me grace, I pray,
That I may clearly see
'twixt holy and profane
What differences there be.

That coming to Your board
I may exalt Your name
Remembering Your grace
Instead of all my shame.

November 2014

Affliction (V)

It is midnight. I was beaten,
But in praise of God my King,
For His wondrous Sov'reign Mercy
In my stocks and chains I sing.

November 2014

Joseph

Though they sold their very brother
And in prison he was thrown
God above him and beyond him
Worked the purpose of His own
That the lives of many people
Might by him protected be,
And the outcome of his visions
In the long run did he see.

November 2014

Outcry

(James 5:4)

Let my wage by fraud withheld
Come before Your holy throne.
Let the cry of my distress
By All-Hearing ears be known.

December 2014

Justice

(Psalm 89:14)

Justice is Your throne's foundation:
Righteousness it rests upon.
You will judge each situation:
Therefore only I go on.

December 2014

I John 3:18

Let me not love in word or tongue,
Mere flapping of the jaw.
Let me instead in very deed
Fulfill the Royal Law.

December 2014

II Corinthians 8:9

O my soul, think upon
The grace of God to thee.
He Who was rich indeed
Took up thy poverty.

He Who deserved great joy,
Delight, applause, and fame
Took up instead thy woe,
Thy misery and shame.

Then let thy praise abound,
And see thou thankful be
For mercy beyond thought
From Matchless Majesty.

December 2014

Colossians 3:2–4

I look alive, but I am dead:
My life is hid away
In Him Who sits upon the throne
And shall return some day.

When He shall come Who is my life
I shall not lowly seem
For I shall share the joy of Him
Who did my soul redeem.

December 2014

The Good Samaritan

'Twas not the Levite or the priest
Who passed by him that day,
But rather the Samaritan
That went upon his way
Who saw his fellow man in need
And could not pass on by.
He loved his neighbor as himself
And did his need supply.
So give me eyes to see the poor,
The weak, the helpless too,
And show the mercy I should show
By imitating You.

December 2014

From Hebrews 12

Come, my soul, gird thee up
And run upon the way
Where the Forerunner went
Upon the darkest day.

The cross thy Lord endured,
The spitting and the shame,
Because He looked beyond
To an exalted Name.

Not unto blood as yet
Hast thou thy sin defied,
And He Who scourges is
Thy Father and thy Guide.

The kingdom that shall be
Forever shall endure.
For that, bear thou the pain:
The joy shall be much more.

December 2014

Into Your Hands

Into Your hands, my faithful God, I place my broken heart.
My foes are fierce, and they have shot me with a fiery dart.
You know the truth of what I say and why this man does lie.
My God, deliver me, I pray, or else, Lord, I may die.

December 2014

Most Gladly Therefore Will I Glory in my Infirmity

I am weak, so very weak.
Pained and foolish, sick and sore.
I will glory in my weakness
For it is my treasure store.

Gold beneath a pile of garbage,
Health behind a sickly pale.
Glory in a pit or prison,
For my Savior cannot fail.

Though I fall, they can't destroy me
Who would seek my soul to harm
For around me and beneath me
Is the Everlasting Arm.

December 2014

Grace is a Diamond

Grace is a diamond, shining bright
Against the backdrop of our night.
Grace is a star, a-twinkling high
Far in the vastness of the sky.
But Grace is more, whose course does run
Across our world, a mighty sun
That warms and lightens all below
Wherever Mercy does bestow
Life where the deadness was before
For Pow'r has Might, but Grace has more.

January 2015

Psalm 70

Make haste, O God to help,
I pray, deliver me.
Make them ashamed that hurt,
Let them confounded be.

Let shame be their reward
Who gloat in wicked pride,
Who say "Aha, Aha,"
For I in Thee confide.

Let those that love Thy name
Forever joyful be.
Let them that love Thy grace
Forever worship Thee.

But I am poor and weak,
I have no strength to stand.
Therefore, make haste to save
And Thy great grace command.

January 2015

I Corinthians 13:4 a

Long did You bear with me
'ere I was born anew.
Long I provoked Your wrath
And did not honor You.

But in longsuff'ring great
Did You give faith and grace
Causing me to repent
That I might see Your face.

Therefore, O give the grace
Of longsuff'ring unto me
That I might mercy show
To those that injure me.

January 2015

They Hated Me Without a Cause

Without a cause they hated You
So small surprise they hate me too.

January 2015

Secret Soldiers: Hymn Version

We all are secret soldiers,
And servants of the Cross,
ordained to pain and sorrow,
to agony and loss.

What cause have we to grumble
when You Who went before
deserving naught but blessing
instead our burdens bore?

Shall flogging, mocking, spitting
deter us from the Way?
What hope had we of glory
had You turned back that day?

It is enough for servants
their Lord to imitate.
Give grace and strength and patience
upon our Lord to wait.

But Oh! The prospect precious
when conflicts all are o'er
to gaze upon the Victor
forever, ever more.

September 2103, cast January 2015 in the plural

II Kings 9:26

You think by lies you conquered me,
Have overcome this day?
But Ahab's blood must wet the soil
Where Naboth's vineyard lay.

January 2015

II Kings 6:16

I cannot see the angel hosts
Of chariots so near,
Yet snorting and the harness bells
I think that I can hear.

January 2015

On Being in the Fiery Furnace Again

From Justice and Integrity
O my soul do not turn,
For those who will not bow shall find
They also cannot burn.

January 2015

Hebrews 5:8

Though perfect in obedience
Yet learned He even more
To walk before Your holy face
Through suff'rings that He bore.

January 2015

I Kings 22:34

I will not raise a hand against you
Nor against you shoot a dart,
But the random arrow flying
Yet will pierce the monarch's heart.

January 2015

Job (IV)

I know not why I suffer
And things distress me so.
But when Your servant suffered
He also did not know.

February 2015

II Kings 19:14

When the enemy shall threaten
With an angry, hurtful word
Let me spread the vicious missive
In the house before the Lord.

February 2015

From Psalm 25
(After P. C. Cragie)

The righteous road is hard;
Around are many foes,
And he who walks this way
Alone his sorrow knows.

So difficult the path
He dare not walk alone:
He needs to walk with him
The God Who is his own.

February 2015

Exodus

Grant me in Your mighty mercy
As I flee across the sea
I may spoil the Egyptians
For the way they treated me.

February 2015

Psalm 28

O be not silent unto me
Lest if Thou hear not when I cry
Like those that perish shall I be
Like those whom Mercy passes by.

Hear when I call upon Thy name
And raise my cry before Thy face.
O rescue me from evil men,
From those devoid of saving Grace.

I pray Thee give them their reward
Who wickedness and falsehood love.
Let Justice visit them in Wrath;
Rain Anger on them from above.

But I will praise my Cov'nant God,
My Strength and Shield and Help alone.
My Sovereign and Protector great,
The God Who is my very own.

February 2015

Grace (IV)

(After John Calvin)

Great is the Grace God gives to men
To meet them in their need
For out of stones He raises up
To Christ a holy seed.

February 2015

Meekness and its Reward

(After Peter G. Feenstra)

What shall you have, O gentle soul
That leaves to God his cares?
What shall you have in Providence
Though you have not earth's wares?

You shall have peace, a mighty store,
And gladness from above,
But more than that you shall have Him
Who now your soul does love.

Let them have houses, boats and cars,
Their pride in which they boast.
But you have more, for you have God
Of treasures great the most.

March 2015

His Yoke is Easy

Yoke me closer to You, Savior,
Keep me safe next to Your side.
Give me Grace to weather trials
That I may in Peace abide.
Give me Meekness for my portion
That I may Your image bear.
Give me steadfast, true Endurance
That I may Your Glory share.
Help me in distress and trouble
That I may cling fast to You.
Bear me up in my distresses
That I may to You be true.
I am weak and full of falsehood.
I am vile and sick and sore.
Grant me Mercy in abundance
For my heart is weak and poor.
I shall not fear that I'll perish,
Fail to come to You at length
For Your arm is ever Mighty
And 'tis You Who are my Strength.

April 2015

A Lesson From Bandit

You silly little dog of mine
That loves each toy and treat,
That looks at me with sad brown eyes
And tells me you would eat

Another treat, more people food
(the treats are hid up high).
You look at me and then at them
And sigh a little sigh.
I wish I looked on higher things
Intently as you do:
More greatly craved the things above,
So imitating you.
To make my joy and great delight
On things unseen be set,
To love intensely what is best,
Just like my little pet.

April 2015

I Must Have It

I found a Pearl out in a field,
Passing beautiful and rare,
Saw its excellence so clearly,
Purely lustrous, wondrous fair.

And if I would have that treasure
I must sell all else beside,
With the proceeds buy that portion
In the which the Pearl does hide.

Let me sell off my possessions,
Let me throw them all away,
Have instead that matchless Treasure
As my own upon that Day.

April 2015

Behold, He Prays

Though beset with very weakness,
Though defiled in many ways,
Still the Master tells His servant
"But behold him, for he prays."

April 2015

Luke 18:1

Dark is the wilderness,
Painful the way
Yet men ought not to faint,
Rather to pray.

Grace in the Father's hand,
Mercy and Love
Wait but to be bestowed
When sought above.

Therefore, be not dismayed
Weak heart of mine.
Pray for the Mercy that
Shall soon be thine.

May 2015

Battle Cry

Against myself I must wage war
Against the world and sin,
Against the powers of wickedness,
Iniquity within.

Must stand against my own intents
As those of old have stood
And conquer evil by the force
Of overwhelming good.

Not let distress turn me aside
Nor faint upon the way,
Not let mistreatment bring me down,
So fail to win the day.

For only he that shall endure
Shall see with joy His face.
I to the end must persevere
By overcoming Grace.

May 2015

I Samuel 21:1

(And David Came to Nob . . .)

Sustain me with the shewbread, Lord,
From out Your holy place.
I flee across the wilderness
Without a resting place.

Show me Your Mercy in distress:
To me grant Grace and Peace,
And help with my besetting sins:
Make my rebellion cease.

That clear before You I may stand
In purity all true,
My spots and wrinkles covered well
By Righteousness from You.

May 2015

The Last Day

This is the world's Last Day,
In microcosm shown
As it shall be the Day
When earth is overthrown.

Creation was the time
The Sabbath Day began,
A day to worship God,
A fitting rest for man.

When they from Egypt came
Across the Red Sea tide,
The day renewed was blessed,
Redemption was applied.

When Christ on earth did walk
He kept the whole day pure,
As all commandments were observed,
His righteousness was sure.

This day did He draw near,
Stretch forth His hands that they
Might see His wounds and know
That Him they must obey.

This day the Church rejoiced
To fall before His feet,
His rising celebrate
As it indeed was meet.

And Christians look ahead
Not to an endless drudge
But Rest and Grace and Peace
From God the Righteous Judge.

This day the Church divides
From worldly task and friend
And looks ahead when He shall come
And bring about the End.

Sweet Lord's Day, bright and fair
That cheers the Christian heart:
A little taste of heaven
That soon will not depart.

Already and not yet,
We taste what yet shall be
When history is o'er
And Jesus' face we see.

May 2015

Built Upon the Cornerstone

I am a little pebble, but You the Cornerstone.
Though fallen in my father, You chose me for Your own.
Upon You built and founded, dependent on Your Grace
You placed me in my setting that I might see Your Face.

A tiny stone and worthless, and yet it pleased You well
To rescue me from darkness, redeem my soul from Hell.
Though now in current weakness, still muddy from the mine,
Eventually in Glory, I shall forever shine.

June 2015

Romans 7:24–26

What I would I do not do:
Just and holy, right and true.
What I do I do deplore
Finding evil ever more.
With the mind I Law obey,
But the flesh is not that way.
Who shall save me from this case?
Who impart sufficient Grace?
Blest be God for Christ His Son
Conqu'ring King, the only One.

June 2015

Acrostic Poem

All creation sings Your praise:
Best their heartfelt chanted lays,
Coming with a skillful song
Down the many ages long.
Every man and bird and beast
For Your pleasure joined at least.
Great the strains they sing unseen
Highest praise, nor subject mean.
In the heavens the angels sing
Just in praise of God their King.
King of mercy and of peace
Limitless Your throne's increase.
Mighty Monarch, still that song
Never shall ages long
Overcome its glad refrain,
Powerful it shall remain.
Quick and dead shall sing as well
Rescued souls from deepest Hell.
Singing their Redeemer's praise
To the end of endless days.
Until earth resounds again,
Very praise shall yet remain
While the church shall ever tell
Xerxes bows, Nebo and Bel.
Yonder sits the Monarch true.
Zion sings, O God, of You.

June 2015

Christ, the King of His People

It is not enough, my Savior, that You conquer Death and Hell,
For sinfulness within me continually does dwell.
I need restraining mercy to correct my faults within,
Suppressing my rebellion and to conquer all my sin.
I need that adversaries, all of them, be overthrown
So that I may come in progress to the safety of Your Throne.

July 2015

And the Books Were Opened

So you lie about my efforts
And accuse me wrongfully?
Do you know the Day is coming
When the whole wide world will see,
When the books are fin'lly opened
And all moral creatures know
Of your guile and sinful falsehood?
For the truth the Records show.

July 2015

Psalm 69

Save me, O God, The waters rise
And overflow my heart.
I sink in mire, I cannot stand.
And tears become my part.

I wait for You. I need Your Grace
My tears have blinded me.
My enemies without a cause
More than my hairs must be.

My mighty foes that would destroy,
They force me to repay
Things that I did not touch or steal
Or wrongly take away.

You know my weakness and my sins.
They are not hid from You.
Let not my brothers be ashamed
Those that to You are true.

For Your sake have I borne reproach,
And shame has covered me.
E'en to my family and my friends
I shall a stranger be.

Your house's zeal did eat me up,
Reproaches fell on me.
I fasted and I mourned but still
Reproach was left to me.

I sat in sackcloth and to them
That drink I was a song.
The mighty in the city gates
With them did sing along.

But as for me, I cry to You,
I beg You hear my cry.
In mercy hearken unto me
Or else, alas, I die.

Deliver me from out the mire
And those that hate me still.
Nor let the deep devour me
Nor pit obtain her will.

I beg You hear, for You are good.
O turn me not away.
Hide not Your face in my distress,
O hear me now this day!

Draw near to me, deliver me,
For You my shame do know.
Reproach my heart has broken and
True heaviness I show.

I looked for some to stand with me,
To me some comfort show,
But none I found who would draw near
And timely pity know.

Let them be dark that hate my soul,
Let them no mercy see.
Pour out Your anger on their souls
Who pain and trouble me.

But I am pained and sorrowful,
O set my soul on high,
Then I will praise You with a song,
With gratitude draw nigh.

Thanksgiving, Lord, shall please You well,
Far better than a beast.
The poor shall hear me and rejoice:
God hears my cry at least.

My God shall save me and His own,
A city full of peace,
His children's children shall dwell there
And endlessly increase.

July 2015

Luke 7:36–45

When You were at the table,
I heard that You were there.
I came to wash Your feet with tears
And dry them with my hair.

I poured upon them precious oil,
A perfume strong and sweet.
And then began in gratitude
To kiss Your blessed feet.

The income of my trespass
Repenting did I pour,
And she the much forgiven
Shall love the Savior more.

You did not cast me from You
But gave redeeming grace
That purified and pardoned,
I may behold Your face.

July 2015

Psalm 70 (II)

Make haste, my God, to help me.
I pray deliver me.
Let them be shamed and silenced
Who would my ruin see.

Confounded, let them be ashamed
Who wrongfully accuse,
Who falsely witness evil
And perjury do use.

Let them be glad and joyful
That love Your holy name.
And such as love Your rescue
Your Majesty proclaim.

But I am poor and needy.
Make haste, my God, to me,
For You are my Deliv'rer.
Let me salvation see.

July 2015

Perseverance (II)

What if this were the world's last day,
Tomorrow Morn arose?
What if the King were manifest
To overcome my foes?

Could I bear up for one more day
In mockery of pain?
Could I discount my mortal woes
In light of Heaven's gain?

Only a few sad seasons more,
Only a few sad hours
And I shall walk the Heav'nly fields
Midst ever springing flowers.

Though I am neither rock nor stone
And have not strength to stand,
I shall arrive in peace at last
Preserved by Mighty Hand.

August 2015

Fear Not

Savior, I am afraid.
My enemies are strong.
They do not hesitate
To do Your servant wrong.

They lie without a pause
And threaten me with harm
And yet I feel nor grace
Nor Everlasting Arm.

You are my God alone.
I beg You to draw nigh.
I beg You to defend
And set me up on high.

O let them be ashamed
That would my soul devour.
O cover me with grace
And overcoming power!

Deliver me, I beg
For I am poor and weak.
You promised You would save
The humble and the meek.

I pray You speedily
To hearken and to hear.
I beg You to protect
And bid me not to fear.

August 2015

Coram Deo

Help me, Lord, in all good conscience
So to live by mighty grace
That I may behave uprightly,
As I walk before Your face.

August 2015

A Bruised Reed Will He not Break

(After John Calvin)

How mighty are Your Gentleness, Forbearance, Meekness, Grace
Who bears with such a one as I when I am in low place.
Instead of putting out my light for love of Your own Name
Instead You fan my embers dim into a stronger flame.

August 2015

On Seeing Birds Fly

Some birds, they flap and struggle hard
to stay aloft above.
But if Your grace should hold me up
my soul should soar in love.
The Wind that blows whereee'er it will,
a strong pneumatic blast,
shall bear me up through all my days
and blow me home at last.

October 2015

Menorah

(For JeAnne)

When in the Tent Your presence dwelt
by cov'ring veil concealed,
without within the Holy Place
the golden lamp revealed
its gentle light from dusk to dawn,
a symbol of Your word,

enlightening the people all
that hearkened to their Lord.
But when the morning sun arose
the lamp did burn no more
for sunlight lit the Holy Place
a-streaming through the door.
So was the richly furnished room
by lamplight dimly lit
until the world's True Sun arose
Himself enlightening it.
In Your light then we see the light
of revelation bold,
New Covenant the truth revealed
that lay hid in the Old.

October 2015

The Comforter

(after Charles Spurgeon)

O my sad soul, how can it be
you are found comfortless?
The foe abuses, and his own
in wrath your soul oppress.
But there is One, the very God,
the Spirit of the Lord
Who comforts you in all your woe
with the almighty Word.
Who shows the things of Christ to you,
your medicine supreme,
Who holds you up in your distress
for Christ did you redeem.

So though this world goes grinding on
and enemies rejoice,
the house of mourning shall be closed
and we with thankful voice
Shall take our places at the board,
at Jesus' wedding feast
and we shall find our tears are dry
and mis'ry gone at least.
He cannot fail His holy task
for Sovereignty belongs
to Him with Father bless'd and Son
for Whom my spirit longs.

October 2015

Samson

In my wretched state and blind,
frightened by a guilty mind
stumbles my soul round and round
til this wretched chaff be ground
Magnify Thy mercy so
that my hair begins to grow.

How Long?

How long, Eternal God,
will You afar remain
while I have sorrow in my heart
and plenitude of pain?

My prayer You don't attend,
my desperate, bitter cry.
But I go mourning day by day
and no relief see I.

But in this wretched state
You caused my soul to see
more clearly than before
my own iniquity.

O look upon my foes
who crushed me cruelly
and charge them for their deeds
in Justice faithfully.

But come, O God, and hear
my deep and bitter cry
for if You help me not,
I fear that I shall die.

November 2015

Hear my Cry

Hear my cry in Heaven, Lord,
Hearken unto me.
Overthrow my vicious foes,
Every enemy.

I am weary, worn, and sad,
feebler every day.
Rescue me, I pray, my God.
else I fly away.

November 2015

From John 15

So deeply cut, so badly hurt
but I read in Your book
the reason that You pained me so.
It was Your pruning hook.

November 2015

From Psalm 56:8

Into Your bottle put my tears
for You have heard my sighs and fears,
but if my rescue is not done
I think You'll need a larger one.

November 2015

From Deuteronomy 8:2–4

Some cry, and You then hearken;
You quickly see and hear,
but I weep night and day at times
for many a long year.

I see the way You led me
through sorrow dark and grim.
I know it was deliberate,
not by caprice or whim.

You made me see my weakness,
iniquity, and shame.
You forced me for my living
to call upon Your name.

I do not understand it,
but yet I bow the knee.
I know that You are doing
the thing that's best for me.

But yet I cannot bear it:
incessant pain and grief.
Before I am consumed, Lord,
I beg You grant relief.

November 2015

From Hebrews 11:32–38

In my distress I cry aloud,
yet those who went before
instead of peace and comfort found
the harsher side of war.
Some stoned, some tortured,
mocked and scourged,
in caves and holes they dwelt
but still their onward way they urged
and could not rest content.
Imprisoned, tempted, scattered, slain,
of comforts destitute,
yet went they bravely on and on
in faith all resolute.

So let me bear this little woe
determined to go through,
to reach the heav'nly halls at last
that I may be with You.

December 2015

From Revelation 6:15–17

Though Him I cannot see
The God Who is my own
in mighty Pow'r and Grace
still sits upon the Throne.

When rocks on reprobates
and hills and mountains fall
those who denied His name
shall meet their Maker all.

It may be not till then
that Justice shall be done.
E'en so I shall await
the judgment of the Son.

December 2015

From Genesis 4:10,11

Let the earth uncover,
let the earth disclose,
blood of innocents once shed
by their wicked foes.

Let not evil men prevail.
Let their wickedness be shown.
Let their ill intentions fail.
Else is Justice overthrown.

Hear, my God, their wretched lies.
See their false pretense and spite.
Judge them or have mercy still
as to You it may seem right.

January 2016

From James 5:10, 11

They pelt me with their lies,
with false and evil claim.
They show themselves unwise,
reviling my name.

For those who went before,
the prophets of the King,
like trials also bore,
bereft of everything.

They patiently endured
through suff'ring harsh and hard,
and when they persevered
received a great reward.

I look for happy days
when trials are no more
for evil men afflict
but only on this shore.

January 2016

For the Rev. Dr. Robert Paul Martin

(after John Bunyan)

I hear the trumpets sound
from golden ramparts high
as to the City fair
the weary one draws nigh,

You served your Lord below,
you fled to Him for grace.
Faith shall be changed to sight:
you shall behold His face.

There shall be no more pain
nor sorrow nor distress.
You shall before the Throne
appear in righteousness.

Come, enter at the door.
'Tis time to end your sighs:
'Tis time to join the Feast
and to enjoy the Prize.

Those whom you leave behind
are safe in Mighty Hands.
He shall provide their needs
for all things He commands.

January 2016

On the Pharisee and the Publican

At the right hand of Majesty
He sits Who bore my shame for me.
Though to the Heavens I dare not look
my guilt is blotted from His book.
In Righteousness, but not my own
fearful I stand before the Throne
but fearless too because for me
was offered up His Majesty.
Not he that struts in sinful pride
is by the Judge thus justified
but he who feels the plague within
and looks for Mercy for his sin.

January 2016

The Last Day (II)

What if this were the world's last day,
the day that brings the end,
beginning too, for those who trust
in Christ shall see their Friend,
In twinkling changed from this sad state
to perfect holiness?
Could I go on a few more hours
in ambient distress?
Come, Life, and overthrow the Grave
and neutralize Death's sting.
Come, Life, and let me righteous see
the Face of God my King.

January 2016

Beside a Death Bed

When Providence my end shall bring,
when ends this mortal strife,
I shall rejoice before my King
for Death indeed brings Life.

Eternal presence of my God,
eternal peace and rest:
These shall be mine when I shall see
Jerusalem the blest.

January 2016

So Teach Us to Number Our Days

Give me, my God, a wiser heart
to number all my days
so that before You I may walk
in all Your holy ways.

January 2016

Small

But wrap a man up in himself
and you will quickly see
how small a package he will make
in his entirety.

January 2016

For the Rev. Dr. Robert Paul Martin (II)

I will remember you
that spoke the word to me.
The outcome of your life
at length I clearly see.

Soon shall you taste of rest,
soon shall your sorrow cease.
Soon know as you are known
and feel a sweet release.

In presence of your God
Whom you have loved unseen,
without impediment,
the veil no more between.

Abundant entrance in
before the Holy One
Who shall receive your soul
and say to you, "Well done."

January 2016

Trust (II)

(after A. W. Pink)

Well may the soul adore
the Holy Trinity
in Glory infinite
and matchless Majesty.

All perfect in all ways,
in Holiness and Grace,
in Wisdom and in Might,
far greater than our race.
If men receive their praise
and accolades from men,
much more does He deserve
the worship offered when
His people come before
His mighty, Holy Throne
to sing the Love and Grace
He showers on His own.
Who is like You among the gods
in Holy Glory grand
in praises frightening
and wonders of Your hand?
Well may the heart rely
on Him, the Mighty King
and at His footstool bow
requesting anything.
No issue is too great,
no problem is too hard,
no need too vast for Him
that does His people guard.
No passion is too strong
for Him to conquer still,
No tempting too intense
but flees one at His will.
No misery so deep
that He cannot relieve.
This is our God, my friends.
In Him we must believe.

February 2016

For C.P.

I am sorry for you, colleague,
though intelligent and kind
All you did has this day perished,
all intentions of your mind.

Had you found the priceless Mercy?
Was with God your life secure?
Sad, I cannot guess the outcome,
only that your life is o'er.

Gone to stand before your Maker,
gone to Judgment's awful hall.
Will your advocate be Jesus?
Has He borne your burdens all?

If not, tragedy is utter
and your ruin is complete,
but if you were found in Jesus
rest perfected at His feet.

August 2015

Hope (II)

We praise You for Your Mercy
but not for that alone.
For Justice pure and Righteousness,
foundations of Your Throne.

For Sovereign Will and Majesty,
For all commanding Power
that guides and orders all our life
e'en at the present hour.

But mostly for Compassion
that gave our Christ to be
both Priest and Offering for us
for all eternity.

Else had we naught to offer
before Your Throne so white,
Ourselves once bound in darkness,
transgressions of the night.

But now we see the Beauty
in Jesus' blessed Face,
not for our own deserving
but out of Sovereign Grace.

The Doing and the Dying
and rising up again
of Jesus Christ, Messiah,
our only hope remain.

February 2016

Genesis 18:25c

The righteous God, He shall do right,
the Sovereign Mighty King,
for He alone plumbs justice's depths
by knowing everything,

the thoughts of men,
their motives dark,
each deed and word within.
He sees the dark recesses of
each fallen creature's sin.
And since we could not save ourselves,
weak through the broken law,
He sent His Son into this world
to suffer shock and awe,
the fiery wrath of outraged God
against our sinful ways.
To Him alone therefore we give
our worship and our praise.
"Praise God from Whom all blessings flow.
Praise Him all creatures here below.
Praise Him above, ye heavenly host.
Praise Father, Son, and Holy Ghost."

February 2016

Psalm 119:50

In my affliction this I find,
a comfort sweet and sure:
His Word has quickened me within
and He shall make me pure.

February 2016

Pilgrim Starts Out

Let me put my fingers, Lord,
more firmly in my ears
and let me run from death's abode
propelled by righteous fears.
Let me ignore the ones who say
that I should still remain
and flee unto the Wicket Gate
for everlasting gain.
The things they sell in Vanity
shall tarnish and decay,
but treasure found in Jesus Christ
can never pass away.
The way is hard and long and lone
but at the end, the Prize,
Who dwells within the city fair
my soul will not despise.

February 2016

The Last Enemy

Our enemy is strong
but he shall lose at last.
Death shall be swallowed up
when this sad world is past.
For when Christ shall return
He shall make all things new.
And you, poor death, shall die
for Life shall conquer you.

February 2016

I Samuel 3:18

It is the Lord. He chose to do
what seemed to Him the best.
Although it hurts, I bow the knee
and in His Gov'r'nance rest.

February 2016

Genesis 15:1

Though I have little in my hand
for things I do not wait,
for I have Christ, and found in Him
my Prize is very great.

February 2016

Death Knocks

When Death shall knock upon your door,
O my sad soul, be not dismayed
for Christ shall bear you safely up
for on His grace your hope is stayed.
The river shall not overflow,
the chilling tide with fearful roll
for Christ is your Redeemer sure
and He shall take to Him your soul.

February 2016

Psalm 119:117

Hold Thou me up, my gracious God,
for on Thee do I cast my care.
In Thee I trust, I, found in Thee,
could not be safer anywhere.

February 2016

East
(After the Rev. Dr. Eric Watkins)

You drove us to the east
Out of the garden fair.
Because we disobeyed
We could not linger there.

For with our fig leaves sewn
Our sins we could not hide.
You covered us with skins
From animals that died.

The angel stood before
The garden entry way
That we should not return
Upon that bitter day.

When from the east your saints
Entered the Promised Land
They met Your Angel bright,
A drawn sword in His hand.

The Tabernacle pitched,
Its door was to the east,
But yet the way was closed
Save unto the High Priest.

Upon the cov'ring veil
Were Cherubim displayed
Because free entry in
Could not as yet be made.

But when upon the tree
Christ offered was for sin
The veil was torn in two
That we might enter in.

We could not save ourselves
From Judgment and the grave.
Forth came the Son of God
For He alone could save.

Blest be the God of Grace
Who would not let us go
But rescued us Himself
That we might glory know.

February 2016

Noah

(After the Rev. Dr. Eric Watkins)

Let me, moved with godly fear
when Your threatenings I hear
flee into Your blessed Ark,
rise above the waters dark.

Safe be found in Christ at last
'til the flood of judgment's past,
else if I Your anger know
I shall drown with all below.

February 2016

Regarding J.I.

I beg You to have mercy
if that might Your pleasure be,
but if not, I pray hang Haman
from the gallows meant for me.

March 2016

Pitch

(After the Rev. James McCarthy)

The blood of Christ so thin
in its viscosity
is still in all its strength
like oily pitch to me
for it seals all the cracks
and leaks my boat contains
keeps judgment's waters out
and all my hope remains.

February 2016

Contrast

(After the Rev. James McCarthy)

How sweet the Gospel is is shown
but only when the wrath is known.

March 2016

From Luke 16

Though Providence gave Lazarus
a meager lot at best
at death the angels carried him
to everlasting rest.

But Dives, who received good things,
more things than tongue could tell,
when he met death, he found himself
in everlasting Hell.

If Providence should seem to smile,
my soul, do not mistake
a temp'ral blessing for the peace
that righteousness can make.

Conversely, if the way is hard
and mercies seem so few,
do not believe because of that
that God is wroth with you.

March 2016

Smokerise

Come, my soul, smell the smoke
that shall forever rise
from burning enemies
who triumphed in their lies.

Unless He mercy shows
forever shall they pay
for scoffing at His Word
and walking their own way.

They were bereft of fear:
they showed themselves unwise
forgetting that He sees,
the One Who made their eyes.

But, my God, smell for me
the Holocausted Lamb,
the Sacrifice once made
for men such as I am.

Be merciful to me
that does Your wrath deserve.
I ask You to forgive
and then my soul preserve.

April 2016

Advocate

(I John 2:1)

Thank God I have an Advocate,
the Son of God on high,
Who, when I sin, He prays for me
that this wretch might not die.

April 2016

Asa

(II Chronicles 16:12)

Let me in my body's pain
Unto my Maker seek,
For though man helps,
He fails to heal
For he is far too weak.

April 2016

Sapphira

(Acts 5:1–11)

Beware, Sapphira, choose to lie
To God the Holy Ghost on high
And it may be that in His wrath
That you may prematurely die.

April 2016

The Last Day (III)

Come, dreadful final day
with darkness and with light.
'Tis Heaven for suff'ring saints;
for sinners, endless night.

Sorrow forever felt
or sorrow felt no more.
Judgment from Him on high
Whom we have walked before.

Justice on all mankind
but refuge found in One
Who bore our sins away,
the gracious, glorious Son.

Sleeping damnation now
wakened again at last.
Mercy for all who trust:
judgment for them is past.

If then the warning call
fearfully you can hear
flee to the Refuge now
then do not bow to fear.

For those in Jesus Christ
Judgment's already o'er.
For all the rest of men
burns anger's bitter store.

April 2016

The Birth of Joy

(Psalm 30:5)

The night was black with darkness,
The pain had no alloy
But with the glorious, rising sun
Was manifest our Joy.

April 2016

Consider the Lilies

(Matthew 6:26–29)

O, my sad, little faith,
Forgetting that He knows
Who clothes the very weeds
And every flow'r that grows.

For color and for grace,
For beauty rich and fair,
E'en Solomon the great
Could not with them compare.

O my sad, little faith,
Behold the birds that fly.
They labor not nor toil,
And I will tell you why.

The Father feeds His birds
Though neither store nor stock
They treasure up, yet still
He feeds the mighty flock.

And shall not Providence
Provide the things you need
If gratitude is in your heart
Instead of grasping greed?

May 2016

Grace

O my soul, think upon
The grace God gives to you.
He bids you to love Him
With faithful heart and true.
He gives what He commands
Or else you sure would fall.
You have more treasure than
The man who "has it all."

May 2016

Behold the Lamb

Come, my soul, look upon
The Lamb that once was slain
Before the world began,
But once and not again.

The blood of goats and bulls
Could never sin remove
But that of very God
Effectual shall prove.

Before the angered Throne
Propitiation made.
All grace is in the Christ.
On Him our hope is stayed.

May 2016

From Exodus 1

(Stanzas 4–6, after Rev. Eric Watkins)

Because the Lord loves Justice,
When men oppress His own
Their cry comes up before Him,
Their sighs before His Throne.

So see, my God, the treatment
My masters gave to me
And call it to remembrance:
O let me justice see.

Remember my distresses,
My agony and pain
And call them to accounting.
O make Your Justice plain.

Because the curse is present
That does not thus imply
That God Himself is absent,
Has passed His people by.

For Faith, the faithful soldier
When understanding fails
Still clings to Revelation
And thus in faith prevails.

The Hope then of the promise
The curse shall overthrow,
And those that died in weakness
Shall Resurrection know.

May 2016

O Ye of Little Faith

O soul of little faith
For what cause do you doubt?
Shall our God promise us
Then fail to carry out?

He says He will provide
The very things you need,
And unlike you, He cannot lie
Or fail His own to feed.

So therefore joyful be
And eat your bread with praise.
He shall provide for all His own
All of their earthly days.

June 2016

On Seeing a Father Comfort a Crying Child

Lord, like a little child
In tears I come to You.
So very oft beguiled,
So very oft untrue.

No reason can I give:
There's no excuse for me.
I pray You show me grace
In mercy rich and free.
O take me in Your arms
And soothe my anxious soul,
Forgiving all my sins:
I pray You make me whole.

July 2016

What Love is This?

What Love is this
That sees my sin
And all iniquity within
And yet gave up God's Son to die
That justly He might justify
And purify and cleanse me so
That I eternal Love might know?

July 2016

The Real Superhero
(for the young sons of the King)

There is one Superhero
that makes all others pale.
He conquered not with sword or gun
but lashes, spear, and nail.

He overthrew all of our foes
by being overcome.
He bore our punishment deserved
that He might bring us home.

If you need someone to admire,
I say let it be He.
You will not find a greater Man
through all eternity.

July 2016

How Long?

Do You in heaven hear my cry
and so regard my deep distress?
How long before You answer me
and deign Your suff'ring child to bless?

July 2016

Veil

O cover me with chastity
as with a wedding veil
awaiting my Beloved's hand
and vow that cannot fail.

July 2016

Orlando

(Ezekiel 33:11 and Psalm 116:15)

Our God does not rejoice
When wicked men depart
But yet His servant's death
Is precious to His heart.

July 2016

Isaiah 40:30–31

Youthful men shall grow so weary,
Fainting shall the young men fall.
He who waits for God to hear him,
He shall soar above them all.

Like an eagle full of power,
As a runner sets his pace
They shall press on to the vict'ry
Who await the Savior's grace.

July 2016

Light of Glory

Upon the mount the bush aflame
Declared the glory of His Name,
So Moses could not venture nigh
Unto the Holy One Most High.

Upon the mount the thunder roared
With lightning glory of the Lord,
And Sinai's law with flame bestowed
The holiness of heaven showed.

Upon the mount the light revealed
The Majesty His flesh concealed,
And whiter than the fuller's art
The clothes the soldiers soon would part.

But when He hung upon the tree
No glory did our blind eyes see,
The flame of Justice, darkly bright
Would rescue us from endless night.

And in the dark His flesh was laid,
The ransom once and fully paid,
For which God raised Him up to live
Where saints and angels glory give.

For death could not with darkness hold
The Prince of Life for sinners sold.
He rose in glorious Majesty
And intercedes for men like me.

So when the darkness seems to gain
Ascendancy in grief and pain,
My soul, recall that Day shall rise,
And you shall see it with your eyes.

July 2016

Shake Well

If Moses shook and trembled so
When to His mountain he did go
Before His holiness revealed
And covenant with blood so sealed,
Then, O my soul, do not mistake
'Tis well before Him that you shake.

July 2016

Hebrews 5:8

Although He were a Son
Yet learned He day by day
Through suff'rings that He bore
His Father to obey.

So what does my soul learn
Through troubles that surround
Except to plead for grace
And mercy to abound?

I need to be upheld.
I have no strength to stand
Unless He holds me up
By Sov'reign, Mighty Hand.

July 2016

Crossing the Red Sea

As I from Pharaoh's army flee
I pray be merciful to me.
Since You are my creator God
Let me the Red Sea cross dryshod.
Since my soul pain and sorrow feels
I pray take off their chariot wheels.
Let my taskmaster's wat'ry grave
Be waves which me from him did save.
Let not oppressors vic'try see.
I beg You come and rescue me.

July 2016

Luke 18:1–8

"Avenge me of my foe!"
So did the widow cry.
The judge, he was unjust
And passed the widow by.

Again she came, again,
And raised the same request.
He pondered what to do
To give himself some rest.

"Though I do not fear God
And men I disregard
I will adjudge this case
And give her her reward.

Lest with her constant pleas
She vex and trouble me."
So he adjudged her case
And listened to her plea.

And shall not God above
When His elect He hears
Avenge them of their foes
And calm their many fears?

For day and night they cry
And though He hears above
In suff'ring long He waits
To save those of His love.

So, my soul, do not faint
But cry by night and day
That mercy be bestowed.
There is no other way.

July 2016

Compassion

(Mark 1:29–31)

(After the Rev. Jim McCarthy)

You saw her where she lay
Ablaze with fever's flame.
You were compassionate
For love of Your own Name.

You drew near to the sick
For Your health unafraid.
You took her feeble hand
And her infection stayed.

You raised her up to stand,
The fever did depart,
So she began to serve
With all her loving heart.

So take, my Lord, my hand.
In misery I lie
With sin and shame engulfed
Almost enough to die.

Because You gracious are
Not that I merit it
I pray You raise me up
And all my debt remit.

And grant me every day
To new repentance know,
To overcome myself
Your graciousness to show.

I cannot save myself.
Therefore to You I flee.
For rescue, Lord, I wait.
Be merciful to me.

July 2016

Canticles 6:3

To Jesus I belong,
My Prophet, Priest, and King,
The fountain of my Joy,
Of Life the Living Spring.

Then do not tempt my soul
With trinkets foul or fair.
Unto my God alone
Allegiance I declare.

O my God, hold me up
That to You I may cleave
And for Your matchless Grace
My wickedness may leave.

August 2016

Intercession (II)

Lord Jesus, pray for me
That my faith may not fail
Through storm of fierce affliction
And misery's sad gale.

Provide for me in life, Lord,
Let Your great grace prevail.
Though sifted in the wind, Lord,
O let my faith not fail.

Uphold me in distress,
And when I death shall meet.
I need Your gracious love
And mercy rich and sweet.

August 2016

Egyptian Gold

Give me not the gold of Egypt.
Give me not their treasure store.
Give me manna with contentment
And I'll ask for nothing more.

Give me what to Thee seems proper
Though it may seem not to me.
Let reproach become my portion
If it comes to me with Thee.

Give me not the leeks and garlic
Or the pot of steaming stew.
Feed me with the bread of Heaven,
Moist me with the Heav'nly dew.

Let the pillar go before me,
"Light by night and shade by day,"
Lead me onwards to the City
By the new and living way.

Lord, I cannot bear this burden:
Therefore hold me up I pray.
And my frame recall with pity,
For I am but living clay.

August 2016

Love

Grant me in Your mighty mercy
Not Your benefits to crave
But instead to love the God-man
Who for me His own life gave.

Blessed Lord, my gracious Savior,
Give me such a glimpse of You
That in loving sweet, submission
I forever may be true.

For my heart is vile and fickle.
And so oft I go astray.
When I savor Your great mercy
By Your side my soul shall stay.

September 2016

Wilt Thou Go With This Man?

Will you go with Christ the God-man
To His holy city high?
Will you yield Him sweet surrender
As to Him your soul draws nigh?

Will you love this gracious Savior
Who for you His own blood shed?
Will you taste of all His goodness
Who's your Lord and living Head?

You can love no sweeter Master,
You can serve no greater King,
Therefore to this gracious Savior
All your love and honor bring.

September 2016

Show me Your Glory

My God, I long to see
As Moses long ago,
Your mighty majesty:
To me Your glory show.

For in the face of Christ
Does glorious beauty shine—
In Justice and in Grace
This Mighty God is mine.

September 2016

For Robert Samuel Dyer

Dear tiny child, you did not see
the light of life on earth
for Death drew near and ravaged you
before you came to birth.

You nothing saw, you nothing knew,
and sorrow deep and grim
you never felt, for God decreed
to take you home to Him.

We bow the knee to Providence
as only Christians can
and wait to meet and greet you, child,
beloved little man.

October, 2016

Fruit

One sows, another waters,
One weeds and rakes the sod,
But increase comes in Providence
Straight from the hand of God.

October 2016

Adoption

What love is this that God bestows
Through Gospel on the men He chose
That sinners might adopted be
And added to His family?

Audacious mystery so great
That sinners from their sinful state
Become instead the sons of God
Though chastened with His mighty rod!

October 2016

From Psalm 46

The mighty God our refuge is
And He in Whom we hide.
When cares and sorrows overwhelm
We safe in Him abide.

He feeds us from His holy place
Whence living waters flow.
Our God provides for all our needs
Who all our needs does know.

Himself makes peace by mighty war
And power strong and great
Nor will He leave us to ourselves
When on His grace we wait.

October 2016

Greater Love

O Greater Love, I pray You rout
The lesser loves from my soul out
That close to You my soul may stay
Beyond the dreadful, final Day.

October 2016

The Tenth Commandment

Give me, O Lord, a heart content
To take what Providence has sent
Without a murmur or complaint
As does befit a real saint.

November 2016

Proverbs 30:8–9

Give me not poverty, I pray,
lest I should steal, profane Your name.
Give me not riches lest in pride
My Savior's rule I should disdain.

Feed me with food enough for me
and, if You please, a little more
that I may share with those in need,
and let me to the end endure.

November 2016

Peace, Be Still

From Mark 4

(After Rev. Jim McCarthy)

The billows are so high,
The boat so small and frail:
I fear that I shall drown
And not in faith prevail.

It seems You are asleep
Upon a pillow lain
While I am in distress,
In agony and pain.

But though You seem to sleep
'Twas You Who led me here
To show my feebleness,
How much I need You near.

I beg You to arise,
Rebuke the tempest high
Since You are God with man,
Our Savior ever nigh.

O let the sea be still,
And let the tempest cease.
Let storm and danger yield
To everlasting peace.

December 2016

Timekeeping

From Daniel 9:21

(After Rev. Jim McCarthy)

Since more than this world do I love
By Grace the things sublime
Then let me set my heart's timepiece
To Holy Temple time.

December 2016

Quietness

From I Peter 3:4

Give me, my God, a quiet heart
That waits in meek humility
Until in Providence You please
In mercy to provide for me.

December 2016

For Robert Samuel Dyer (II)

Dear tiny child, that never saw
The sun rise or the evening fall.
It was God's hand that took your soul,
Your body weak, and O so small.

He spared you sorrow and distress,
He chose you should not evil know.
He chose to give you greater rest
Than men who live long years can show.

October 2016

Provision

How my God will provide for me
I cannot even guess,
But quietly I wait upon
My Father's faithfulness.

For with means or without them
Or against them it may be,
He promised that He would provide:
I shall provision see.

No man can learn to be abased,
To wait before the Throne
But he whose heart belongs to God
And hopes in Him alone.

December 2016

Unbelief Trampled

(From II Kings 7:2)

He scoffed at God's sweet promise,
The obstacles too great,
But saw the famine broken
When trampled in the gate.

December 2016

Subdued

(From Mark 5:1–20)

After Rev. Jim McCarthy

I was so very, very wild,
So long perverse,
So oft defiled
Until He came across the sea
That He might mercy show to me.
No pow'r could break my chafing chains

But His Who tempests wild restrains.
So then delivered, clothed, and still,
Subdued unto His gracious will
O let my happy chorus be
"Hear what the Lord has done for me."

December 2016

On Christian Education

How great the mercy You bestow
Upon both old and young
That our old ears may hear the truth
Upon a child's tongue.

December 2016

Looking Upwards

I feel the pow'r of creeping Death
Grow stronger every day
But Heav'n within my heart remains
And brightens all my way.

December 2016